Endangered Species

Look for these and other books in the Lucent
Overview series:

Endangered Species

by Sunni Bloyd

LUCENT
B·O·O·K·S

LUCENT *Overview Series* OUR ENDANGERED PLANET

OUR ENDANGERED PLANET

Library of Congress Cataloging-in-Publication Data

Bloyd, Sunni.
    Endangered species.

    (Lucent overview series)
    Includes bibliographical references.
    Summary: Describes how and why various species of animals and
the tropical rain forests are threatened with extinction and discusses
the importance of ensuring their survival.
    1. Endangered species—Juvenile literature. 2. Nature
conservation—Juvenile literature.   [1. Rare animals. 2. Rare plants.
3. Conservation of natural resources]
I. Title. II. Series.
QH75.B59 1989   333.95′16   89-12895
ISBN 1-56006-106-5

To my mother, who truly could talk to the animals.

Contents

INTRODUCTION

The Vanishing World

When billions of passenger pigeons darkened the sky overhead, it was hard to imagine that someday they would be gone. Later, when hunters killed millions of buffalo for their hides, they had no idea that the buffalo would be reduced to only five hundred animals. Today, we still find it hard to believe that the world's wildlife is disappearing.

We can visit the cougar in his lair or swim with the whale in the ocean simply by turning on the television or opening a magazine. Because we see and hear so much about wild animals, it seems that they are safe and all around us. But in fact the plant and animal population of our world is vanishing at the rate of 100 species per year, a rate that is expected to increase to 100 per day by the year 2000.

The United States Fish and Wildlife Service lists 531 species as endangered (in danger of extinction) or threatened (not yet endangered, but likely to become endangered in the future) in the United States. The World Wildlife Fund reports that at this very moment more than 1,200 species of birds, fish, and animals are endangered throughout the world. Nearly 25,000 plant species are on the brink of extinction. In the United States alone, almost 700 native plants face extinction by the year 2000.

We're just beginning to understand that the world community of plants, animals, birds, and fish is kept in balance by the many species within it. An individual species is an important part of its ecosystem—

the community of all the living things as well as the soil, air, and water within a habitat.

Like a piece of fabric that is made up of many strands of thread, life on earth is made up of many living things, each closely related to the others. Remove a strand of thread from a piece of fabric, and the cloth will be weakened. Remove many strands, and the cloth will fall apart. In the same way, the loss of one or two species seems to do little harm, but the loss of many can have serious consequences.

The beaver is a good example. Once beavers built dams all over the American continent, trapping water laden with topsoil in their ponds. Over time, the beaver ponds filled with soil. When the beavers moved on, the ponds dried up, leaving rich, farmable topsoil.

European settlers came to North America. They discovered that their crops grew well near rivers. They did not realize that beavers were responsible for the rich soil there or that beaver dams prevented floods. The settlers trapped the animals and sold their hides to make hats. Soon there were very few beavers left in North America.

The beaver is brought back to the country

Rivers and streams ran more swiftly because there were no beaver dams to slow them. Millions of tons of topsoil washed away from forests, meadows, and farmlands. Farmers' crops did not grow as well in the poor soil left behind. In some places, the lack of beaver ponds caused wells to go dry. People in the city and the country did not have enough water. Finally, when the value of the beaver was understood, efforts were made to bring it back to the countryside and restore the balance of nature.

Understanding the relationship of all living things has taught us that a threat to the survival of one species is a threat to other living creatures, including ourselves. For example, scientists discovered the hazards of DDT, a pesticide that nearly wiped out the bald eagle, when they noticed its harmful effects on birds. Then DDT turned up in the milk children drank. The government banned the pesticide to protect humans as well as wildlife. Whether pollution, toxic waste, overpopulation, or some other hazard threatens wildlife, we have learned to pay attention to it because we share the same environment.

There are many practical reasons to preserve wildlife. We depend on trees and vegetation, most of them in forests, to recycle carbon dioxide into the oxygen we breathe. Wild plants and animals provide us with food, medicines, and commercial products from shampoo to floor wax. Hunting, trapping, and fishing are important wildlife industries that provide a livelihood for many people. New crops and livestock can be developed by crossing domestic strains with hardier wild varieties. And tourism to wilderness areas gives developing nations desperately needed income.

Yet there are other valid reasons for saving the plants, animals, birds, and fish of the world. Some people find the sheer beauty of nature a good reason. Others feel that killing living things for no reason is wasteful. Still others think it is arrogant for us to claim the whole world to do with as we please. Perhaps all of these reasons motivate the thousands of people who are working to save endangered species.

This book tells how species become endangered and what steps are being taken to protect them. It uses the stories of several species— some that became extinct, some that recovered from near-extinction, and some that are still in danger—to show how people play a major role in the destruction of plant and animal species, and what we can do to save them.

CHAPTER ONE

Hunting the Passenger Pigeon

On March 24, 1900, a boy took the BB gun he had received as a Christmas gift and went out into the Ohio countryside. The young hunter had no particular quarry in mind. Probably he hoped to bag a fat partridge or rabbit for the family dinner table.

The boy was an excellent marksman. In a short time his game bag contained several small animals.

All at once a single pigeon fluttered into sight. The boy stealthily moved closer, aimed, and fired. The pigeon fell dead with a BB in its brain.

The young hunter, proud of his accomplishment, gathered up his trophy. It was a kind of pigeon he had never seen before, so he brought the bird to a friend who was an amateur taxidermist. (A taxidermist preserves the skins of animals, birds, and fish and stuffs them so that they can be displayed.) She recognized the species of the bird. It was a passenger pigeon, the last one ever shot in the wild.

The name of the boy is unknown. It does not really matter, for he was not responsible for the disappearance of a species that had numbered in the billions when European settlers first came to North America. He only did what thousands of others before him had done: take a little of the bounty of nature.

The passenger pigeon made its home in the forests between the Atlantic Ocean and the Great Plains of North America. It was once the most numerous species of bird in the world. In 1808 Alexander Wilson, an early American naturalist, saw a flock of at least 2,230,000,000 (two billion, two hundred thirty million) passenger pigeons in Kentucky. John James Audubon, who studied and drew pictures of birds, watched a flock pass overhead continuously for three days in 1813. He estimated that a billion birds had flown over him every three hours.

Passenger pigeons migrated across the forests of North America, feeding on mast (wild berries, grains, and nuts that had fallen to the forest floor). The birds nested in colonies and traveled in huge flocks that darkened the sky as they passed. Witnesses compared the passage of a flock to a storm. Strong air currents, whipped up by the wings of millions of birds flying as fast as sixty miles per hour, chilled the air. Bird droppings fell like hail. When a flock came to rest for the night, groups of birds roosted together in such numbers that trees collapsed under their weight.

The passenger pigeon's nesting season lasted from mid-April to mid-May. The nesting area sometimes covered several hundred square miles, but the birds were always crowded together. Every tall tree was filled with as many as a hundred nests. The floor of the forest was soon covered with droppings, so the flock often had to fly as far as fifty miles to find food.

Hunting the passenger pigeon

No one, not even naturalists like Audubon, thought the passenger pigeons could die out. They seemed to be an endless resource. At first, settlers followed the Indians' habit of collecting only fat squabs (half-grown pigeons) that had fallen to the ground. Because these young birds wouldn't have survived anyway, the species was not harmed. Later, hunters shot adult pigeons as well as squabs.

But the worst damage was done after 1850, when nearly five thousand professional hunters, called pigeoneers, developed ways to kill the birds in great numbers. They notified one another by telegraph

Famed nineteenth-century naturalist and artist John J. Audubon classified and painted numerous species of birds. The wildlife conservation group, The Audubon Society, was named after him.

when a migrating flock was sighted. They used captive birds, called stool pigeons, as decoys, and set out nets to entangle the wild birds. Sometimes they put out grain soaked in alcohol to disorient the birds that ate it, making them easy prey. Pigeoneers cut down trees full of nests or lit sulphur fires under them to suffocate nesting birds. Millions of birds were killed and shipped to eastern markets over the newly built railroads each year.

Pigeon hunting remained controversial

Naturalists and game protection clubs, realizing that the pigeon was threatened with extinction, tried to restrain the pigeoneers. But few people shared the naturalists' belief that the pigeons were in danger. Shortly after the last great passenger pigeon migration— through sparsely settled territory near Petoskey, Michigan, in 1878—E.T. Martin, a game dealer in Chicago, defended the hunting in a pamphlet.

> This whole pigeon trade was a perfect Godsend to a large portion of Emmet County. The land outside of Petoskey is taken up by homesteaders who, between clearing their land, scanty crops, poor soil, large families, and small capital are poorer than Job's turkey . . . and in years past have had all they could do fighting famine and cold, and but a year or two [ago] all Michigan was sending relief to keep them from starving. . . .
>
> The ''pirates and bummers'' [who hunted pigeons] left some $35,000 in good greenbacks right among the most needy of these people. Many were enabled to buy a team, others to clear more land . . . and this money did more to open up Emmet County than years of ordinary work. [The money pigeoneers paid for food, lodging and supplies] put scores of honest, hard-working homesteaders on their feet; it increased trade, and if sent by a special act of Providence, could not have done more good.

Martin wrote, ''The pigeon will never be exterminated [killed off completely] so long as forests large enough for their nestings and mast enough for their food remain.'' Because the birds were migratory, he felt they could care for themselves. Their nesting grounds in the wilds of Canada and the Indian Territory would save them from extinction. He thought the passenger pigeon was created to benefit people, as much an item to be bought and sold as wheat, corn, hogs, cattle, or sheep.

Many shared Martin's opinions, but they were wrong. The continued settlement of North America spelled doom for the passenger pigeon through destruction of its habitat (the place that provides everything a plant or animal needs to live and grow).

The forests where the pigeons nested and roosted were cleared for farming. The pigeons could no longer find mast to eat. They ate seed

Just over a century ago, passenger pigeons numbering in the billions darkened North American skies. That they could become extinct seemed impossible—yet the last one died in 1914.

corn as it was planted and cleared the fields of ripe grain before it could be harvested. Farmers considered the birds pests and wanted them killed.

Although many passenger pigeons remained in the 1890s, hunting had broken up the great flocks. Scattered into small flocks and pairs, the passenger pigeons could not nest in colonies. Few produced young. Diseases spread by domestic birds thinned their numbers still further.

In spite of rewards totaling over one thousand dollars for the discovery of a nest or colony, the passenger pigeon could not be found in the wild after 1900. Only a few birds remained in zoos and private aviaries. Martha, the last passenger pigeon, died in the Cincinnati Zoo in 1914.

The passenger pigeon became extinct at a time when many people in the United States began to think about conserving nature. Naturalists and those who enjoyed the wilderness realized that the passenger pigeon had died out because of uncontrolled hunting and the destruction of its habitat. They began to study wildlife and tried to save other species that were threatened, such as the buffalo.

Why the passenger pigeon became extinct

The passenger pigeon became extinct for several reasons. The simplest reason is that people killed more pigeons than the natural reproduction rate could replace. Hunters thinking only of profit killed a million birds a year, and those who settled the birds' habitat encouraged the extermination because they didn't want to be bothered by the huge flocks.

Another reason is loss of habitat. In clearing the American continent, settlers cut down the forests of beech and oak that had provided food and nesting sites for billions of birds. Without them, the great flocks could not continue to exist.

A third reason is that passenger pigeons did not reproduce successfully after hunting broke up their normal social organization.

Passenger pigeons lived in colonies. They cooperated in raising their young. Older birds taught inexperienced birds how to build nests and care for the squabs. Without the help of a colony, the pigeons built poor nests. Most of the squabs fell to the ground and died. When only scattered birds remained, they usually failed to breed. Passenger pigeons had few instinctive behaviors to help them find mates outside a colony. They needed the closeness of many other pigeons to stimulate breeding.

A fourth reason is that passenger pigeons died from diseases carried by domestic birds, that had been imported from other countries. People trying to breed passenger pigeons in captivity lost many of the endangered birds to diseases they had no immunity to.

The passenger pigeon became extinct because of factors still threatening many species today: commercial exploitation, competition with farmers, destruction of habitat, and disease caught from introduced animals. For species still alive the solution to these problems means the difference between extinction and survival.

Extinction as a natural process

At this point someone might ask, "What's the difference if one species of bird dies out? Extinction is a part of nature. Look at the dinosaurs." It's a question that deserves answering.

First, the loss of a single species is important because it weakens the ecosystem within which that species lived. Each species provides others with shelter, food, water, or some other necessity. Removing a single species can set off a chain reaction that affects many others. Scientists estimate that one disappearing plant can take up to thirty insects, animals, and plants with it.

Second, the loss of one species reduces the genetic diversity of its ecosystem. Each animal, plant, insect, or fish has its own set of inherited genes, that control its growth, reproduction, and other functions. When there are many different species in an ecosystem, scientists say it has genetic diversity (a variety of genes).

ROTHCO
ORIGINAL

Ecosystems need genetic diversity to help them survive changes in the environment. For example, scientists have found that wilderness areas with many different species recover better from pesticide spraying than areas with few species. While one species dies out or declines, another is able to survive and take its place. But if the number of species is already reduced, the whole ecosystem is in danger of collapse when faced with environmental change.

Third, the extinction of the passenger pigeon was hardly a natural process. Extinction is normally a gradual process that occurs when a species doesn't adapt to a changing environment. Dinosaurs became extinct over millions of years. The elimination of species like the passenger pigeon, which took only a few decades, is really extermination, not natural extinction.

The main reason for this type of extinction is direct competition between humans and other species. Humans compete with animals for living space and the earth's resources. As more and more people fill the globe, the wildlife that remains experiences more and more pressure.

Why passenger pigeons were important

Passenger pigeons played an important role in their ecological community. Their loss weakened the whole.

Flocks of migrating passenger pigeons helped preserve and renew the forests they passed through. They made room for other plant and animal varieties by nesting and roosting in such great numbers that they broke down the trees. In addition to mast, they ate insects damaging to forest trees: grasshoppers, beetles, ants, and caterpillars. Their droppings spread seeds from the berries they had eaten and fertilized the soil so new plants could grow.

Although the farmers didn't know it, killing off the passenger pigeon caused predators (animals that hunt and kill other animals for food) to attack their livestock. Wolves, cougars, and foxes hunted passenger pigeons as their natural prey (animals hunted or killed by other animals for food). When their major source of food disappeared, they turned to cows, sheep, and poultry.

Some naturalists believe that passenger pigeons could have adapted to living in smaller groups if they hadn't been killed off so quickly. They might have bred in captivity if there had been time to learn exactly what conditions they needed in order to reproduce.

Passenger pigeons, larger and meatier than domestic pigeons, were as popular at nineteenth-century dinner tables as chicken is today. If properly managed, the flocks might have provided food for generations of hungry Americans. No one will ever know, because all these possibilities became impossibilities once the passenger pigeon died out.

CHAPTER TWO

The Buffalo Come Back

One fall day in 1907 a crowd of cowboys, settlers, and Indians gathered near a railroad in the dusty Oklahoma town of Cache. The Indians were the most excited members of the crowd. Some had come long distances by foot for the occasion. Many wore their finest tribal regalia. Among them were chiefs of several tribes and women carrying papooses on their backs.

The buffalo were returning to the Oklahoma prairie after many years. Travelling in a special stock car, fifteen head of buffalo would soon arrive at the newly created wildlife preserve in Cache. It was the first national preserve created to save an endangered species.

While they waited, the older Indians told the younger ones what it was like when the buffalo ranged their land. They described great buffalo hunts and the many uses their tribes had for the buffalo.

Seas of buffalo

Scientists have traced the buffalo to the Pliocene epoch, the last warm period before the Ice Age. About twenty-five thousand years ago prehistoric bison crossed a land bridge in the Bering Strait between Asia and North America. (Although most people call the familiar shaggy animal buffalo, its scientific name is bison.) Fossil remains can be found on both sides of the Bering Strait. Scientists think that the bison traveled both ways over the land bridge, some staying on each continent when the land bridge disappeared beneath the ocean.

The bison that remained in Asia developed into the European wisent, the North American buffalo's closest relative. Smaller and not so shaggy as the buffalo, wisents have only a small hump.

The bison that stayed in North America adapted well to the Great Plains. Two subspecies (closely related types) flourished. The woods bison lived in the mountainous Northeast, while the more numerous plains bison roamed the Great Plains.

Early explorers found it hard to describe the buffalo herds. One said, ''There is such a quantity of them I do not know what to compare them with, except with fish in the sea.'' Another said, ''The plains were black and appeared to be in motion,'' as a single herd passed by.

Indian cattle

When first seen by Spanish explorers in the sixteenth century, the buffalo was king of the North American continent. Between thirty and sixty million buffalo ranged from Canada to Mexico and from West Virginia to Oregon. The shaggy beasts the Spaniards called Indian cattle covered the plains. The explorers could ride for days and never be out of sight of them. Such vast numbers provided an abundant food supply for the Indians living on the plains.

The Plains Indians depended upon the buffalo. It provided shelter and clothing as well as food. They called it *Tatonka*. For most Plains Indians, *Tatonka* represented the Great Spirit and played a large role in their religion.

The Indians had a use for nearly every part of the buffalo. They ate its meat, including the tongue, blood, brains, intestines, fat, and stomach. They fashioned hairbrushes from the rough side of its tongue, and canteens from its bladder. From its hide, the Indians made robes, shirts, dresses, belts, moccasins, caps, and mittens. They

The buffalo represented life itself to the Plains Indians. The Indians hunted the buffalo for food, used its skin for clothing and shelter, and its bones and horns for tools and ornaments.

covered their teepees with buffalo hides, and also used hides to make blankets, cooking vessels, and buckets. From buffalo horns, they made spoons, ladles, and ceremonial masks. Whole buffalo skulls became religious altars. Bones were used as arrowheads, scrapers, paintbrush handles, and counters for gambling games. Buffalo tails became fly whisks and knife sheaths, and sinew was made into twine, bowstring, or arrowhead wrapping. Buffalo hair was braided into rope or used to stuff balls for Indian games. Even buffalo chips, dried buffalo dung, served the Indians as fuel for their fires.

New markets for buffalo meat and hides, and the development of railroads soon brought white hunters to the buffalo herds. Men unemployed after the Civil War flocked to the plains during the 1860s. Nearby towns welcomed the buffalo hunters. Storage yards for hides, and meeting places for buyers sprang up near the railroad tracks.

Many factors encouraged the killing of buffalo. To settlers and railroad men, buffalo were huge, hairy pests. Normal structures could not withstand their urge to scratch themselves. Buffalo rubbing against one settler's new log cabin collapsed it overnight. They knocked over so many telephone poles that the company installed special spiked collars around the poles to discourage them. (It turned out that buffalo *preferred* to rub against the spiked poles.) Migrating herds blocked trains and trampled cultivated lands. Hunters told themselves they were only killing off the excess buffalo. There were plenty more out on the plains.

The United States government, then in a bloody war with the Plains Indians, encouraged the slaughter by supplying free cartridges to buffalo hunters. So much the better if the hunters exterminated the Indians' walking grocery store!

Buffalo crazy

Suddenly in 1872 the whole West went buffalo crazy. Men quit their jobs to hunt buffalo. They figured that killing a hundred buffalo each day would provide a monthly profit of six thousand dollars, triple the salary of the president of the United States. That year between ten thousand and twenty thousand buffalo hunters invaded the plains.

The hunters developed a way to shoot buffalo that left all the carcasses in one location. They called it the stand. An accurate and powerful new rifle, the Big Fifty Sharps, made it possible to kill a large number of buffalo without stampeding them. A hunter planning a stand located a separate group of between twenty and seventy buffalo. Then he walked toward them upwind (so that they could not catch his scent), taking care to stay hidden. When he was only two hundred yards from the buffalo, he killed the most active animal.

The confused herd moved about, but only a few animals tried to escape. The hunter picked off the buffalo that moved out of the herd. Firing one shot per second (any faster caused the rifle barrel to melt), he could kill the entire herd by leaving the calmest buffalo for last.

Some hunters tried to kill record numbers of buffalo, even though the skinners and butchers that followed them could only handle a little over a hundred buffalo a day. The remaining carcasses were left to rot. A buffalo hunter named Tom Nickson killed 3,200 buffalo in thirty-five days.

An estimated million buffalo a year were slaughtered between 1870 and 1883. The vast herds had withstood blizzards, floods, and the attacks of Indians and wolves. Yet they could not survive this campaign

Unlike the Indians, white hunters often killed buffalo just for sport. No one dreamed that the thundering millions of buffalo would soon be only an echo of the past.

of extermination. By the 1880s millions of tons of bones littered the plains that had once been covered with buffalo. Finally, even the bones were shipped east to be used as fertilizer and china. Of the buffalo themselves, only a few hundred remained.

The Plains Indian culture was shattered by the loss of the beast that had provided the necessities of life. Starvation forced the proud and warlike people to surrender to the U.S. government and accept life on the reservation.

Saved from extinction

In 1886 William Hornaday, chief taxidermist at the U.S. National Museum, realized that his collection did not contain any buffalo. He quickly arranged a trip to collect some before the species became extinct. After two trips to Montana, Hornaday returned home with twenty-one, including a large bull. His exhibit of stuffed buffalo was highly praised when it opened.

A year later, another museum sent an agent to the same area to obtain buffalo skins for its collection. Not one buffalo could be found. The failure of this expedition shocked scientists and buffalo hunters alike. Where had all the buffalo gone?

In January 1889, Hornaday sat down with pencil and paper and listed all the buffalo he could account for. He knew of fewer than 100 free-ranging buffalo in the United States. Additional buffalo survived under lax federal protection in Yellowstone National Park, and there were a few more in zoos and private herds. The number totalled barely 1,000 buffalo! Hornaday grimly predicted that no wild buffalo would be left in ten years.

Sadly, his prediction came true within eight years. Even the "protected" herd at Yellowstone dwindled under constant poaching (illegal hunting) as taxidermists offered fifty dollars and more for a buffalo head, no questions asked.

During the winter of 1893, poachers killed 116 buffalo that had wandered beyond the park boundaries. Only 20 survivors remained

An Indian medicine man prays for the buffalo to again grace the land with its magnificent presence. The Indians knew that the world was not complete without the buffalo.

in Yellowstone. (The entire United States held only 540 live buffalo.) The incident aroused strong national support for the preservation of the Yellowstone herd. Congress finally passed an effective law forbidding the killing of buffalo.

In spite of efforts to build up the Yellowstone herd, by 1904 most buffalo were in private hands. Realizing that the future of the shaggy animals was insecure as long as they could be sold or slaughtered at their owners' whim, journalist Ernest Harold Baynes launched a campaign to establish government-owned herds.

The American Bison Society was formed in 1905, its purpose to preserve the buffalo. William Hornaday, who had devoted much of his life to the buffalo, was chosen president. Baynes served as secretary. Theodore Roosevelt took the position of honorary president.

Thanks to the American Bison Society, in 1907 Congress appropriated fifteen hundred dollars to stock the first federal buffalo range, eight thousand acres of prairie in the middle of what was once Oklahoma's Indian reservation. This herd proved successful, and other federal preserves soon followed.

In the 1950s ranchers across the United States began to raise the buffalo for its low-fat, low-cholesterol meat. Within thirty years over 100,000 buffalo roamed North America's parks, zoos, and private pastures.

Getting along with the buffalo

There is more to saving an endangered species than merely increasing its population. The buffalo is a good example of the problems that arise after a species recovers from near extinction.

Because buffalo are restricted from their former range to smaller, protected areas where there are few predators, buffalo preserves are overpopulated. Excess animals must be butchered or sold for breeding. Some people want buffalo hunts to reduce the numbers. Other people oppose the hunts.

Another problem is that buffalo in the parks carry tuberculosis

Small herds of buffalo roam national parks in the western United States today. Conservation practices have allowed the buffalo, or bison, to make a comeback.

and brucellosis, serious illnesses that can infect domestic cattle. Disease is a natural way of controlling overpopulation, but these sicknesses could spread to nearby ranches or kill off all the park buffalo. Some people recommend allowing such diseases to run their course. Others want to vaccinate the buffalo against them. Still others, mainly ranchers, want to destroy infected herds. Because of the danger they pose to livestock, buffalo that wander out of park boundaries are usually shot.

The buffalo's habit of straying onto highways or into towns near buffalo preserves poses a hazard to human life and property as well. Whether they wander because of ancient migratory instincts or because the grass is greener on the other side of the freeway, being outside the preserves brings them into conflict with humans. Buffalo are, after all, large and unpredictable wild animals. For the safety of humans, livestock, and the buffalo themselves, the big, shaggy beasts must be kept within preserves.

Wherever wild animals live near humans, similar problems arise. They must be solved to the satisfaction of conservationists and local residents if wildlife preserves are to have the support of all.

CHAPTER THREE

One Foot in the Grave

It was nearly dawn. Several biologists sat silently in a Wyoming sagebrush plain, holding spotlights pointed at a group of burrows. They had been there all night, waiting. Tonight they were lucky. A black-masked head popped out of a nearby burrow, then instantly withdrew. It was a black-footed ferret, the most endangered animal in North America.

The biologists brought a small trap and placed it in the burrow. The next afternoon they removed it with the ferret inside. The year was 1982, and the biologists were beginning an investigation into the habits of a species that many had thought extinct. In fact, less than 150 of the critically endangered animals still existed, all of them at this location. Soon this ferret would be wearing a radio transmitter collar that would tell researchers about its activities.

The elusive black-footed ferret

A member of the weasel family, the black-footed ferret sports a black mask across its eyes, black feet, a black-tipped tail, and a beige body. About the size of a mink (between eighteen and twenty-four inches long), it weighs from one-and-a-half to three pounds. Its main prey is the prairie dog, a rodent that looks like a ground squirrel.

Black-footed ferrets live in prairie dog burrows and are active at night. That makes them very hard to find. Often the only evidence of a ferret is the trench it makes when removing dirt from its burrow. If biologists find such a trench, they return at night with spotlights and wait to see if the animal that made it is indeed a black-footed ferret.

Although black-footed ferrets were first seen a hundred years ago, scientists knew little about them. In 1964, scientists discovered a small group of them in South Dakota. Unfortunately, this group of ferrets disappeared just as biologists were beginning to study them.

For nine years no one could find a black-footed ferret. Wildlife experts began to think the species might be extinct. Then one day, near Meeteetse, Wyoming, a dog killed a strange-looking animal. The dog's owner took the animal to a taxidermist who called the Wyoming Game and Fish Department. The mystery animal was a black-footed ferret.

Studying an endangered species

Excited biologists began to make plans. They did not want to harm the ferrets. Using European ferrets as stand-ins, they developed safe ways of trapping and handling them.

Researchers had to be very careful. Canine distemper is so contagious among ferrets that an entire colony could die if people accidentally brought the disease in on their shoes or hands. Dogs were banned from the area. Biologists disinfected themselves before touching the ferrets. Anyone who felt ill stayed away because ferrets can also catch human diseases. Everyone handling a ferret wore a surgical mask.

Once an adult ferret was trapped, it was anesthetized, weighed, measured, and fitted with a small radio transmitter on a collar. A numbered tag was also put in its ear to identify it. After it recovered from the anesthesia, the ferret was returned to its burrow.

Scientists fitted eighteen ferrets with radio transmitter collars. The transmitters allowed scientists to learn when the animals were active and where they went.

The biologists needed to know how many ferrets there were. They

A black-footed ferret surveys its sagebrush domain. Scientists are working hard to keep ferrets, perhaps the most endangered species in America, from becoming extinct.

watched the prairie dog town at night with spotlights, recording how many ferrets they saw, especially those with ear tags. They trapped all the ferrets in selected areas, tagged their ears and released them. A short time later the biologists returned to trap all the ferrets in the same areas, once more tagging and releasing them. By comparing the number of untagged ferrets with the number of tagged ferrets, they could estimate the total population. According to those estimates, 128 black-footed ferrets remained of a species that had once occupied over a hundred million acres in the grasslands of central and western North America between Canada and Texas.

The grassland ecosystem

The disappearance of the black-footed ferret was not the result of a deliberate campaign of extermination. The ferret was not slaughtered for its meat or its coat. It threatened no one except prairie dogs. The ferret simply got in the way of those who did not understand the close relationship between the members of the grassland ecosystem where it lived. It was an innocent bystander in a war that nearly destroyed it.

Before the arrival of European settlers, the American grasslands existed as a vast community of species that depended on one another. Buffalo, prairie dogs, and ferrets played important parts in the life cycle of the grassland ecosystem.

After buffalo ate the grasses in an area, prairie dogs moved in, digging burrows. They compacted the soil with their feet to build a mound at the entrance of each burrow.

Black-footed ferrets moved into some of the burrows. They, along with other predators, kept the prairie dog population from growing too large. By killing the sick or weak prairie dogs, they kept the colony healthy.

Buffalo came to prairie dog towns and rolled in the loose earth to remove insects and shedding hair. Once buffalo chose a wallow, or rolling spot, the prairie dogs moved to another part of the prairie dog town. By tearing up the burrows, buffalo kept the prairie dog

Dave Beletski and Tom Campbell weigh a ferret in a trap. They are so concerned for the ferret's well-being that they wear surgical masks to protect it from their germs!

town from spreading out. Abandoned wallows quickly grew over with grass, and the cycle would start again.

After the buffalo disappeared, settlers brought in livestock to graze on the rich grass. The life cycle of the grassland ecosystem was broken. Without buffalo to break up their burrows, prairie dog towns

A young ferret yawns as if to say it's bored by all the fuss the humans are making about it. Happily, people are realizing that without delightful creatures like the ferrets, the world would indeed be a boring place.

spread out. Some stretched for miles. Because settlers killed off the larger predators, small predators like the black-footed ferret could not control the prairie dog numbers.

Cattlemen said prairie dog burrows were hazards to horsemen and livestock. They complained that prairie dogs ate grass that cows or sheep could have eaten. The cattlemen poisoned the prairie dogs by the millions. Even prairie dog towns on public lands, such as parks and military bases, were poisoned so that livestock could be pastured there.

The poisons cattlemen and government officials used to kill prairie dogs were nonselective. Their effect was not limited to a certain species. Any animal or bird that ate them was poisoned. Black-footed ferrets and other animals scavenging the carcasses of poisoned prairie dogs were themselves killed by compound 1090 or strychnine. Because they lived in prairie dog towns, ferrets also died when poison gas was pumped into the burrows.

Disaster strikes

By 1983 all that could be found of the black-footed ferret was the single colony in Wyoming. But scientists were hopeful. The number of ferrets in the colony seemed to be growing. Perhaps there would soon be enough to transfer some to areas where they used to live. Establishing separate colonies would lower the risk of disease wiping out the species.

A few ferrets were brought into a research center in Sybille, Wyoming for a captive breeding program. In the wild, endangered species sometimes have trouble finding a mate. At the research center, scientists could help the ferrets reproduce.

But in 1985 disaster struck. Suddenly there were only fifty black-footed ferrets in the prairie dog town. Somehow, distemper had invaded the colony, perhaps carried by a skunk or coyote.

Worse luck followed. All six ferrets in the captive breeding program

Veterinarian Dr. Tom Thorne carefully handles a caged ferret inside a research laboratory. Researchers will fit the ferret with a radio-transmitter collar so they can keep track of the ferret's activities after it is returned to the wild.

died of distemper. Now the only ferrets left were those in the distemper-ridden prairie dog town.

Conservation officials had to make an agonizing decision. They could leave the ferrets alone and hope some survived, or they could bring all of them into captivity. They decided to bring the ferrets into the research facility.

Then a whole new series of problems arose. The ferrets had to be trapped. They needed new buildings where they could be kept completely separate from one another until it was certain they were free of disease. Caretakers had to be hired and trained. Money had to be obtained to finance the new project. And the scientists who worked there had to figure out how to help the ferrets successfully breed and raise young.

In the end, after a year of searching, only eighteen healthy black-footed ferrets were rescued. The species clung to existence by the narrowest margin. Could the best efforts of the research team bring it back?

In 1987 help came from the Moscow Zoo in the form of six Siberian ferrets, a species closely related to black-footed ferrets. Six more Siberian ferrets came to Sybille from other parts of the United States. By studying the breeding behavior of these ferrets, researchers found ways to help black-footed ferrets reproduce.

Happily, the effort was a success. During the first breeding season, two litters of black-footed ferrets were born at Sybille. The following year thirty-eight more babies were born. In 1988 a second breeding colony was established at Wheatland, Virginia. A third colony will soon be established in Nebraska. Scientists are proudly looking forward to the day when there will be five hundred breeding pairs of black-footed ferrets in the world, and the little masked animal that nearly became extinct can be reintroduced into the wild to once more become a part of the grasslands community.

CHAPTER FOUR

Saving the Tiger

A trip to the zoo just wouldn't be complete without a stop at the tiger exhibit. Something about the big, orange-and-black-striped cats attracts us. Is it their beauty, their grace, or their wildness? The fact that tigers are powerful predators causes us to both fear and admire them.

Today the tiger is protected as an endangered species. Its picture decorates calendars, book covers, and sweatshirts. It has become a symbol of the grace and beauty of wild animals.

But tigers were not always considered beautiful or admirable. In countries where tigers lived, they were feared and hated. People killed them whenever they could. The story of our changing relationship with tigers reflects our changing attitudes toward all wild animals.

Tiger subspecies

Tigers first appeared in Asia nearly two million years ago. Over the course of thousands of years, geographic barriers, such as high mountains, separated small groups of tigers. They developed into several subspecies.

There are five subspecies of tiger alive today. Each lives in a different geographical region. The Siberian tiger, the largest subspecies, lives in the Soviet Union, North Korea, and China. The oldest subspecies, the South China tiger, inhabits remote forests in China. Sumatran tigers live only on the Asian island of Sumatra. Corbett's tigers roam the dwindling jungles of Malaysia. The most numerous, the Bengal tiger, can be found across Indian, Nepal, Burma, Bangladesh, and China.

The tiger hunter who wanted to save tigers

At the beginning of this century, India had one of the largest tiger populations in the world, over forty thousand. Tigers whose preferred prey is humans killed hundreds of people each year. It's no wonder the public considered anyone who killed tigers to be a hero. It was the fashion to display trophies, rugs, coats, and even bedspreads made from tiger skins.

The most famous tiger hunter, Jim Corbett, killed hundreds of these tigers during this time, when India was a British colony. In years of tracking the most dangerous tigers, Corbett developed a great respect for the species.

He became the first tiger conservationist. Although tigers sometimes killed people, Corbett felt the species was too magnificent to exterminate. Since tigers and people could not live safely together, he thought the only way to save the big cats was to set aside some land just for them.

Few people agreed with Corbett's ideas. As in other countries, tigers in India came into conflict with humans when people cleared the forests and built villages near their habitat. Many tigers killed livestock. Some came into villages and attacked children. Villagers and government officials felt that the more tigers that were killed, the better.

When India became independent, forests were cut down for new villages and industry. Overgrazing and poor farming methods took nutrients from the soil. Irrigation, power, and industrial projects damaged the forests. As its habitat was destroyed, India's wildlife disappeared.

By the early 1970s, India's tiger population had dwindled to eighteen hundred. The Indian people now agreed with Corbett. The tiger *was* too beautiful and wonderful to destroy. The Indian government made it illegal to kill tigers.

The government launched Operation Tiger in 1972. The program had two goals. First, it aimed to establish a population of tigers that could survive in the wild. Second, it wanted to preserve the wilderness for the Indian people to enjoy.

Protecting the tiger

Unrestricted development of the countryside had weakened the Indian forest ecosystem. To protect the tiger, the government would have to protect its habitat as well. Suitable tiger territory had to be set aside for it, and populations of the species that tigers prey upon had to be increased. The government would also have to find ways

A Bengal tiger glides as easily through the water as through the jungle. Protecting the tiger's habitat is as important for its survival as protecting the tiger itself from hunters.

to make the new system beneficial to the villagers who lived nearby, so that they would support the tiger preserves.

Under Operation Tiger, sixteen parks were created as tiger sanctuaries. With help from the World Wildlife Fund and other conservational groups, the Indian government spent millions of dollars and set aside thousands of acres for tigers. Because small groups of animals in patches of wilderness easily die out, the preserves are large.

Officials hoped that tigers would reproduce and spread out to areas where there were no big cats. The plan worked. Today India has about four thousand wild tigers.

Enough land for tigers and humans

Like Corbett, conservationists planned to keep tigers and people apart. In the core area of each preserve, villagers are not allowed to pasture cattle or cut trees. Here the tiger can hunt or raise its young undisturbed. Around the core is a buffer area where prey flourishes. Local people fish, gather honey, and collect wood or grass in the buffer area. The soil around the villages is poor, and the villagers depend on these forest products for extra income. Surrounding the buffer is a mixed-use zone, where logging and grazing are allowed. Deer, the tiger's favorite prey, graze there too. In this way both tigers and humans benefit from the preserves.

Tourists come from all over the world to visit the tiger preserves. Each year more than thirty thousand visitors come to Corbett National Park, the first and most famous tiger preserve. From the backs of elephants they hunt tigers with cameras instead of rifles.

Tourism benefits the people who live near the tiger preserves. It creates jobs in the hotel, restaurant, souvenir, and forestry industries. Local people work as guides or game wardens in the preserves or make souvenirs for tourists.

However, tigers still threaten villagers. As the population of tigers increases, the number of victims grows. In 1972, eighteen people were killed by tigers. By 1988, the yearly total had climbed to sixty.

The tiger's beautiful coat makes it a prime target for poachers. Its large size and ferocious nature make it an object of fear as well. How tigers and humans can live together in harmony is a difficult problem for conservationists to solve.

Those who have lost a family member to a tiger want the big cats controlled. If the problem can't be solved, Operation Tiger may fail.

A tiger is indeed a dangerous neighbor. The Bengal tiger averages 9½ feet long and 450 pounds. One of the largest cats on earth, it's such an efficient hunter that biologists call it a superpredator.

Except when raising young, tigers live alone, hunting red deer and wild pigs that live in the forest. If villages are nearby, they prey upon livestock grazing at the forest edge.

When its habitat is intact and there is plenty of prey, a tiger usually fears and avoids humans. But when people move into its territory, or when there is no food, a desperate, old, or wounded tiger will hunt humans. Once it has killed a human, a tiger is likely to attack humans again.

These tigers kill villagers who come into the forest, lying in wait where they've seen people before. Villagers are not allowed to carry weapons into the forest. Large sticks are their only legal defense against instant death. Yet if a villager kills a tiger, he can be fined or put in jail.

It's thought that tigers learn to eat people when villagers kill off their normal prey. Now there is more prey in the tigers' habitat. Conservationists hope that tigers will return to eating deer and wild pig.

Other conservationists believe that tigers attack humans when they are not allowed enough undisturbed territory. They say that when the core, buffer, and mixed-use land zones are maintained, tigers do not harm their neighbors. It does seem that the worst problems occur where villages are inside the buffer zone, or villagers go into the core area of a tiger preserve.

Tigers may think people are deer

Several attempts have been made to solve the problem. Because tigers attack humans from behind, scientists think they may mistake them for grazing deer. The government has issued brightly colored masks for villagers to wear on the back of their heads when they go into the forest, so that tigers will recognize them as humans. Electrified dummies dressed like villagers have been set up to shock tigers, teaching them to avoid people. Known people-eating tigers are captured and relocated to zoos. Still tigers continue to kill people.

Operation Tiger began with the idea that humans and tigers could both survive if each had their own place. However, as tiger and human numbers increase, it's becoming harder and harder to keep the two species apart. Other countries trying to solve the same problem look to Operation Tiger as a model program. If it fails, the tiger may become extinct in the wild. Even if Operation Tiger succeeds in saving the Indian tiger, other measures must be taken to insure the survival of all tiger subspecies.

Tigers are internationally recognized as an endangered species. Experts think there should be at least two thousand of each tiger subspecies to ensure its survival. Most subspecies are far below this number and seem likely to continue to decrease. In the wild, groups as large as a hundred animals can simply disappear through disease or genetic flaws.

"CHIEF, WE'VE LOCATED BIG FOOT AND I'M AFRAID HE'S NOT AS DUMB AS WE THOUGHT!"

This government storeroom is nearly filled with the skins, horns, and tusks of animals killed illegally by poachers. People's desire to possess products made from rare or exotic animals makes poaching a real threat to many species' survival.

Because tigers are so close to extinction, an international tiger Species Survival Plan has been developed to save them. First, all the tigers in the wild were located and counted in 1987. This world survey found around eighty-four hundred wild tigers, most of them Bengal tigers. Of the rarest subspecies, the South China tiger, only twenty to thirty remain in the wild.

Now each group of tigers is being evaluated. What threatens them? Could they become extinct in the next five, twenty, or fifty years? If so, how might this be prevented? The study looks at what prey animals are available, conflicts between tigers and humans, humans' use of tiger habitat, and local projects that affect tigers. This information will help governments make better decisions about conservation.

Agreements are being made with each country about what to do if a group of tigers approaches extinction. Together, scientists and government officials are deciding when to introduce new tigers from wild or captive groups. They are planning when wild tigers should be brought in for captive breeding. The Species Survival Plan calls for making these decisions before a crisis occurs.

Zoos help save the tiger

Tigers and other exotic animals have always been popular exhibits at zoos and parks. When it became difficult to buy wild tigers, zoos began to keep records of the locations and pedigrees (ancestry) of tigers in captivity. They used this information to decide what tigers to mate together.

Not every zoo shared information, so the pedigrees and locations of many tigers were unknown. Zoos with rare subspecies of tigers had an especially hard time finding suitable mates for them.

Zoos with rare tigers needed to find unrelated tigers for breeding, so that their cubs would be healthier, with less chance of faulty genes. When breeding within a small population, it is important to mate individuals that are not closely related. Genetic diversity helps living things fight off disease and protects them against inherited defects.

The Species Survival Plan surveyed all the zoos and parks in North America and Europe to discover how many tigers of each subspecies are in captivity and if their ancestry is known. About fourteen hundred tigers are now in Western zoos, five hundred of them in North America.

This information is being published for zoos to use in planning their breeding programs. Zoos with rare tigers can now find mates for them. They can trade tigers, so that the tigers they breed will not be too closely related.

The survey found that many zoo tigers are of unknown or mixed ancestry. Some are crosses between Bengal and Siberian tigers, for example. Under the Species Survival Plan, most zoos have recently agreed not to mate such tigers. The number of spaces for tigers in zoos is limited, and this will leave more room for rare tigers.

By cooperating, zoos can maintain healthy tigers of all subspecies. They can even increase the numbers of rare tigers, like the Sumatran tiger. Perhaps someday these tigers will be used to restock areas where wild tigers have died out.

CHAPTER FIVE

The Disappearing Rain Forest

In a way, tropical rain forests are an endangered species—perhaps the most important of all. Rain forests are ecosystems, groups of plants and animals that work together to survive, and their disappearance threatens the species that live within them. But that is not all. Because rain forests recycle carbon dioxide into oxygen and thus control the world's climate, they are vitally important to every living thing. Yet they are vanishing so quickly that they may be irretrievably lost by the end of the next century.

In the time you can read this sentence, eight acres of tropical rain forest will have been bulldozed and burned out of existence. Every minute twenty-five to fifty acres vanish. Agriculture, logging, and cattle ranching are destroying the rain forest forever.

Inside the rain forests

Tropical rain forests are tall, dense jungles growing along the equator. Brazil, central Africa, and the islands between Southeast Asia and Australia hold the biggest rain forests.

Inside the rain forest, trees, vines, and other plants become very large. They grow together to form the canopy, a mass of intertwined branches a hundred feet above the ground. It shuts out almost all the sunlight.

Many animals, birds, and insects live in the canopy. Although tropical forests cover only 7 percent of the earth's surface, over half the world's species of plants and animals live in them. (Scientists think there are around 5 million species in the world, but only 1.75 million have been identified.)

If the destruction of the rain forest continues, 750,000 species will become extinct by the year 2000. During the next century, one-third of *all* species will vanish—more than 1.6 million kinds of birds, fish, plants, insects, and animals. Most will disappear without having been studied.

The rain forests' ecosystem

Hundreds of thousands of species thrive in the rain forest. However, the soil beneath it is too poor to support continued cultivation. Most tropical forests are thousands of years old, descendants of forests that lived before the Ice Age. Over the centuries, rain has washed away most of the soil's nutrients, the elements needed for the life and growth of plants or animals.

Rain forests evolved to keep these nutrients from washing away. The dense forest canopy shuts out the sun and wind. It keeps the temperature at about seventy-five degrees. Plants living in the rain forest add to the high humidity. Because it's so warm and moist, most of the rainfall returns immediately to the air as vapor. What remains is absorbed by fallen leaves and decaying matter called forest litter. Bacteria and fungi thrive in the warm, damp rain forest. They break down the forest litter into elements that can nourish life. A dense, shallow mat of roots captures these nutrients, allowing very little to wash away or sink into the soil. Most of the nutrients remain in the rain forest's plants and in the first few inches of soil.

Native people have lived in the rain forests for thousands of years without destroying them. But today too much rain forest is being cut down. In poor, overcrowded countries, jungles are a source of wealth. The governments of such developing countries hope the jungles will provide homes for the homeless, food for the hungry, and resources to sell to other countries.

Careful development of the rain forests could lessen the damage, but often short-term rewards come before the need for preservation. Destructive agricultural methods, logging, cattle ranching, illegal wildlife trade, and dams built to provide electric power are destroying the rain forests.

The most serious threat is agricultural expansion. More and more settlers have entered the rain forest in the last fifty years. They are trying to survive in a time of explosive population growth and economic difficulty.

Most of these settlers use slash-and-burn agriculture, a way of

A man works to clear an area of rain forest for agriculture. The expansion of agriculture is the most serious threat to the survival of the rain forest.

farming that was developed when few people lived in the rain forest. Those who use slash-and-burn agriculture clear small plots of land. They cut down and burn the forest. After two or three years of cultivation, the nutrients in the soil are used up. Then the farmers clear new plots of land.

Allowing the forest to return

In the past, farmers cleared their new land at a distance from their old fields. The forest surrounding the little plots soon took them over again. After about fifteen years the farmers returned to the old land that had been left to the jungle, and found they could farm it once more.

But today's settlers do not allow the forest to return. They clear the land in huge strips, beginning at the edge of their old farms. No jungle vegetation is left to spread back over the old farmland. Day by day the farmers move deeper into the rain forest, cutting down and burning the vegetation. They cut down so much of the jungle that it can't recover.

Logging is the second most destructive activity in the rain forest. Ten million acres of forest are cut down each year. Most of the wood is used as firewood or charcoal, the chief fuel of the developing world. The wood is also used to make buildings and tools. The most valuable kinds of wood, such as mahogany, are sold to other countries.

Loggers use two methods of felling trees: clear cutting and selective cutting. Clear cutting is the most destructive method. It removes all the trees in an area. Selective cutting, felling only certain trees in an area, is almost as destructive. Trees within the jungle are connected by vines and supported only by shallow root systems. When one tree is cut down, others come down too. Selective cutting damages as much as two-thirds of the trees in a region.

Logging harms the rain forest in other ways. The heavy equipment used for logging causes damage along the roads. Logging roads invite farmers and others to move into the heart of the forest.

A strip-mining operation reduces the once lush jungle to a scarred and barren mudflat. Strip mining, as the name indicates, strips off a shallow layer of earth to yield the mineral ores below the surface. This practice destroys large tracts of forest land.

Cattle ranching also harms the rain forest by exposing the soil to erosion. In Central and South America, millions of acres of rain forest are converted to pasture each year. Because the soil is poor, the cattle cannot find enough to eat. Tropical rains wash away soil exposed by overgrazing.

In addition, trade in endangered species is stealing plants and animals from the rain forest, even though international laws forbid it. There is a market in wealthy countries for birds, plants, and items made from endangered species. Poachers strip national parks and reserves of endangered plants and animals that play important roles in the ecosystem.

Hydroelectric dams also cause many problems. Harnessing rivers to provide power for industry and jobs for a poor population seems like a good idea. But when dams are built in the rain forest, they flood and kill the jungle. People and animals living nearby must find new homes. Heavy rains fill the streams and rivers with silt—topsoil that rain has washed away. The rivers and streams must be dredged so that enough water passes through the dam to produce electricity. The electric generators themselves can be ruined by silt in the water. For these reasons hydroelectric dams aren't as successful in the tropics as they are in other places.

Each of these activities contributes to the rapid disappearance of rain forests. If they continue, within eighty years there will be no healthy rain forests left.

Why rain forests are important

The death of the rain forests means the extinction of hundreds of thousands of animals and plants, many unknown to science. It means the end of a fragile and beautiful ecosystem that has existed for hundreds of thousands of years. For some people, this is reason enough to save the rain forests. But there are other reasons that are even more urgent.

Rain forests are an important part of our planet's balance of nature. They provide much of the world's oxygen by recycling carbon dioxide. They recycle rainwater when tropical forest plants draw water from the soil and release it as vapor. Eighty percent of the rainfall in tropical climates comes from water recycled in this way. Finally, rain forests cool surrounding regions because they absorb more of the sun's energy than open land does. Without the tropical forests, the temperature would rise. Polar ice would melt, raising ocean levels. Farmlands would dry up.

By soaking up heavy tropical rain and releasing it slowly, rain forests also provide a steady source of water. Cutting them down would let heavy rains run off all at once, causing floods in the rainy season and drought in the dry season.

The plants and animals of the rain forest provide unique medicines and products. Drugs from the rain forest are used to treat malaria, convulsions, and headaches. Researchers hope to find cures for cancer and heart disease by studying rain forest wildlife. Millions of dollars worth of other products come from jungles each year, too. Rattan, bamboo, spices, pesticides, waxes, shampoos, and steroids contain ingredients from the rain forests. Untold riches will be lost if the forests disappear.

Native cultures will vanish with the tropical forests. Lacking education to prepare them for good jobs, people from the rain forest will be forced into the poorest parts of the cities. Their knowledge of forest plants and animals can be of little help to them there. It, too, will disappear as their children learn the ways of the city instead of the ways of the forest.

Saving the rain forests

Could the rain forest be saved by putting all its species in zoos or botanical gardens? The answer is no. The rain forest is a complete ecosystem. It must be preserved as a whole.

A question that biologists and the World Wildlife Fund are trying to answer is "How much forest must be saved?" About 4 percent of all tropical forests are protected as national parks and preserves, but this may not be enough. Many species need home ranges far larger than the typical preserve or park. In the Amazon River Basin in Brazil, biologists are trying to learn how big an area of tropical rain forest is needed to support all the plants and animals that live there. Then they can help plan the right size for national parks.

Any plan for saving the rain forest must help solve the economic problems of the people that depend upon it for their livelihood. Only by giving them alternative ways of making a living can conservationists convince them to stop cutting down the rain forest.

Environmentalists are developing industries that do not harm

A section of rain forest smolders after being burned by farmers. This ruined section of forest is only a small example of the destruction taking place in one of earth's most important ecosystems. The rain forest provides a habitat for thousands of plant and animal species. It also renews the earth's oxygen supply.

tropical forests, but do earn as much money as clearing land or logging. One day, instead of destroying the rain forest, those who live in it may collect vines and rattan, tap rubber trees, or collect samples of plants to be studied. Improved forest management and more plantations growing wood for fuel could lessen the damage being done by logging and give villagers a source of income.

Developing nations must buy expensive manufactured goods from countries like the United States and Japan, while they have only raw materials such as lumber to sell. They often can't afford to set up extensive parks or research projects. One solution is to give countries that establish such programs "conservation credits" to pay off international debt.

Expensive international aid projects like dams harm the environment. Instead, conservationists suggest smaller local projects, such as experiments in raising crops and trees together.

Although the rain forest is threatened, its future is far from hopeless. Through these and other constructive strategies, progress is being made toward saving this unique ecosystem for future generations.

CHAPTER SIX

In Defense of Endangered Species

Human activity has been the cause, whether deliberate or accidental, of the disappearance of hundreds of species. Thousands more are threatened. It is a responsibility we must bear. We can no longer blame the decline in our wildlife on "natural causes."

The problems of habitat destruction, exploitation, and pollution are not limited to one country or continent. International cooperation and legislation are necessary to solve them. Many countries, including the United States, have committed themselves to protecting endangered species in every part of the world. Conservation groups such as the International Union for the Conservation of Nature and Natural Resources, World Wildlife Fund, and The Nature Conservancy take part in global programs to save endangered species.

The Endangered Species Act of 1973

In 1973 Congress recognized the need to protect endangered species by passing the Endangered Species Act. It reads in part:

The Congress finds and declares that—

(1.) Various species of fish, wildlife, and plants in the United States have been rendered extinct [because] of economic growth and development untempered by adequate concern and conservation;

(2.) Other species of fish, wildlife, and plants have been so depleted in numbers that they are in danger of or threatened with extinction.

(3.) These species of fish, wildlife, and plants are of esthetic, ecological, historical, recreational, and scientific value to the Nation and its people;

(4.) The United States has pledged . . . to conserve . . . the various species of fish or wildlife and plants facing extinction.

The far-reaching programs of the Endangered Species Act are designed to preserve threatened wildlife and help it return to self-sufficiency. Under the Endangered Species Act, the federal government, all fifty states, conservation organizations, individual citizens, business, industry, and foreign governments take part in preserving wildlife throughout the world.

The act gives the secretary of the interior, acting through the U.S. Fish and Wildlife Service, broad powers to protect all forms of wildlife in danger of extinction. The secretary of commerce, acting through the National Marine Fisheries Service, has similar authority for most marine life.

As of August 1988, as a part of the Endangered Species Act, more than five hundred native mammals, birds, reptiles, crustaceans, plants, and other life forms were officially protected on the U.S. List of Endangered and Threatened Wildlife and Plants. Additionally, more than five hundred foreign species were listed.

The listing process

Anyone can nominate a species for listing as endangered or threatened. Species that are listed receive government protection because they have been added to the official list according to the rules of the Endangered Species Act.

The act classifies protected species as either endangered or threatened. An endangered species is in danger of extinction throughout all or a significant portion of its range, or home territory. A threatened species is likely to become endangered within the near future. Fish and Wildlife Service biologists often propose species for listing, but a suggestion can also come from individuals, organizations, states, or scientists.

When a species meets the standards for federal protection, a proposal to list it is published. This proposal, called a rulemaking, begins the official process of including the species in regulations that protect endangered and threatened species. These regulations have the effect of law and apply to all U.S. residents. The rulemaking is published in the Federal Register, a daily government publication. Then public meetings are held to give interested parties a chance to express their concerns and opinions about the proposal.

After a review of what was said at the meetings and any new information, the Fish and Wildlife Service decides whether the candidate species is endangered, threatened, or not in need of federal protection. If the final decision is that protection is needed, the rulemaking is published again, and the listing as "endangered" or "threatened" becomes official. Listed species cannot legally be harmed, pursued, hunted, transported, or traded in interstate or foreign commerce without special permission.

Are all endangered species being helped?

The listing process is lengthy and expensive. Lack of government money causes a backlog of species waiting to be investigated. Conservationists grumble that there are more species awaiting listing than there are on the official list. They fear these unprotected species may become extinct while the government delays. Still, a great many species benefit from government protection.

A species can be delisted as well. Delisting, official removal from the list, occurs when the species no longer needs protection. Perhaps the species has recovered from danger, or new information might show that it isn't really endangered after all. Or the species might have become extinct. Of twelve species removed from the Endangered and Threatened list in 1987, four species were determined not endangered. Only three had recovered. The three were species of birds from the Palau Islands in the western Pacific: the Palau dove, the Palau fantail, and the Palau owl. Five species had become extinct.

A species is reclassified when conditions change. Recently the chimpanzee was reclassified from threatened to endangered because of the continuing destruction of its habitat. Delisting and reclassification follow the same formal rulemaking procedure as listing.

Critical habitat

The Endangered Species Act also calls for the protection of critical habitat—areas of land, water, and air needed by an endangered or threatened species for survival. Thus, critical habitat includes breeding

ROTHCO
ORIGINAL

"FRANKLY, PROFESSOR, I THINK WE'RE THE ONLY
ENDANGERED SPECIES AROUND HERE!"

Captive whooping cranes await the day of their release into the wild. Whoopers usually lay two eggs. But since they will only raise one chick, scientists take the extra egg to hatch in captivity. They hope this technique will increase the number of cranes enough to ensure the survival of this severely endangered species.

sites, shelter, and room for normal behavior and population growth. Areas are designated "critical habitat" by a process similar to rulemaking.

The main threat to critical habitat is uncontrolled land or water development. The federal government itself carries on, either directly or indirectly, a great deal of development. So the law requires all federal agencies to make certain that their projects do not threaten a listed species or harm its critical habitat.

Recovery

The goal of the Endangered Species Act is to restore listed species to self-sufficiency. A species recovery plan, similar to the Species Survival Plan but limited to the United States, is prepared for each listed species. The plan may suggest purchasing critical habitat, captive

Patuxent Wildlife Research Center in Laurel, Maryland, has raised over a hundred whooping crane chicks to adulthood. The big birds are then returned to their natural habitat in the Midwest. The Patuxent program has been very successful in saving whoopers from extinction.

breeding, or new research. One of the program's most spectacular successes came with the whooping crane, which dwindled to fewer than twenty birds in the late 1940s.

Female whooping cranes usually lay two eggs but rear only one chick. Scientists removed the ''extra'' eggs and incubated them at the Patuxent Wildlife Research Center in Laurel, Maryland. This produced a healthy captive flock of whooping cranes.

Feeling that a second wild flock with a different migration path would increase the whooping crane's chances of survival, biologists then tried something totally new. They transplanted whooping crane eggs to the nests of greater sandhill cranes, which were not endangered. The sandhill cranes raised the little whoopers as their own. Today the transplanted whooping cranes migrate with sandhill cranes to a winter home far from their true parents. If something should happen to one of the flocks, the remaining flock of whooping cranes will still survive in the wild.

The program has paid off. The total number of whooping cranes has reached more than a hundred and continues to grow.

The Endangered Species Act and the Lacey Act (which forbids importing any animal taken illegally from wild habitat in another country) commit the United States to an international treaty that regulates the sale and purchase of endangered wildlife. This treaty, the Convention on International Trade in Endangered Species of Wild Fauna and Flora (CITES), has now been signed by nearly one hundred countries.

CITES protects endangered species around the world by making it illegal to sell them across international boundaries. It is intended

Poachers killed this rhinoceros just to get its horn. Some people prize rhino horn as a magical substance they believe gives them power. The huge sums that they will pay for it are too much for poachers to resist.

to stop poachers from killing or capturing endangered animals in one country, taking them to another country, and selling them there.

Before CITES, poachers could capture rare monkeys in South America, then ship them to the United States or Europe, where zoos and research institutions would pay high prices for them. Now it is illegal to import endangered species. South American poachers have no market for their monkeys.

Unfortunately, not all the nations that have signed the CITES agreement enforce its regulations. The rhinoceros is rapidly approaching extinction because dealers will pay nearly any price for its horn, and some countries continue to allow it to be sold.

Rhino horn is purchased for two purposes. Folk healers in the Far East use small amounts of it to treat fevers. Aspirin might be just as effective, but people don't want to change. But a greater danger to the rhinoceros is the Middle Eastern custom of wearing daggers with rhino-horn handles. Ninety percent of the illegal trade in rhino horn finds its way to the small Middle Eastern country of North Yemen.

In North Yemen the most important sign of an adult Muslim man

A rhinoceros horn sits on the shelf of an Oriental "pharmacy." Oriental folk medicine prescribes powdered rhino horn for various ailments and weaknesses. It is believed to provide strength.

These Middle Eastern daggers have handles of carved rhino horn. Even at the staggering price of fifteen thousand dollars apiece, their popularity has driven the rhinoceros to the brink of extinction.

is the ceremonial dagger, or *jambia*, that he wears at his waist. His family gives it to him when he reaches the marriageable age of twelve to fifteen years. Once, only the elite rich could afford daggers with rhino-horn handles. But during the 1960s and 1970s wealth from North Yemen's oil wells raised even poor men's expectations. Although there is not so much oil money now and it is illegal to import rhinoceros horn, *jambias* with rhino-horn handles are still easy to find. There are always buyers for the daggers, even though they cost over fifteen thousand dollars apiece.

In Kenya in 1970 there were 20,000 black rhinos. By 1985 Kenya's black rhino population had declined to only 425. In the same time, the price of rhino horn on illegal world markets soared from 35 dollars for about two pounds to over 500 dollars. The same devastation of rhinoceroses took place in Africa, India, Java, and Sumatra.

The explosion in the price of rhino horn in the 1970s made poaching a profitable business. Well-organized gangs of professional poachers armed with automatic weapons replaced the occasional village poacher. These professional poachers have wiped out the rhino wherever they could find it.

Rhinos are now too few and scattered to breed successfully. When they do produce young, the poacher is waiting for them. In Kenya the government has decided to create special sanctuaries within national parks where the rhino can be safely bred in captivity. Other countries are trying to decide what to do to save the rhino, but time is running out.

TRAFFIC

CITES authorities and conservation groups are doing their best to stop illegal trade in endangered species. World Wildlife Fund has set up a special network of agents, called TRAFFIC, to support the CITES agreement.

TRAFFIC calls attention to violations of wildlife trade laws. Through programs on radio and television as well as books and articles in magazines and newspapers, TRAFFIC informs the public about countries that allow trade in endangered species. It notifies law enforcement officers about illegal shipments. TRAFFIC also sponsors special projects that educate the public about the laws protecting endangered species.

Protecting endangered species is the law. By educating the public about the laws and seeing that those who break them are punished, CITES and TRAFFIC defend thousands of species of plants, fish, birds, and animals.

CHAPTER SEVEN

Helping Endangered Wildlife

Many organizations around the world are working to preserve endangered species. (Some are listed at the back of this book along with their addresses, if you would like to write to them for more information.) Some are global in their approach, some are local. Your neighborhood may even have its own group.

But there are really only three ways organizations can approach the problem of saving endangered species. Some associations, like the World Wildlife Fund (WWF) and its sister association, the International Union for the Conservation of Nature and Natural Resources (IUCN), take a worldwide view. Others, like The Nature Conservancy (which focuses on maintaining biological diversity), deal with a single issue. Still other groups, such as Operation Oryx, concern themselves with saving one species at a time.

Who stands up for endangered species?

World Wildlife Fund is the leading private U.S. organization working worldwide to protect endangered wildlife and wild lands. Its annual budget runs over twenty-two million dollars. WWF approaches conservation on a worldwide scale, lending its expertise and financial support to programs around the globe. Its top priority is protecting the earth's biological diversity through conservation of the tropical forests of Latin America, Asia, and Africa—home to most of the world's species.

WWF supports people and groups who carry out practical, well-planned, and scientifically-based conservation projects. Since it first began in 1961, WWF has taken part in more than 1,300 projects in 104 countries, using a wide array of conservation methods.

WWF programs are intended to:

1. *Protect habitat.* WWF has assisted in the establishment and management of 185 national parks and protected areas, helping developing countries to conserve the full range of their biological resources.

2. *Protect individual species.*

3. *Promote ecologically sound development.*

4. *Support scientific investigation* that provides information to allow informed conservation and development decisions.

5. *Educate people in developing countries* to build local support and understanding of conservation issues.

6. *Train local wildlife professionals* to guide conservation in their own countries.

7. *Encourage developing countries to design, fund, and carry out effective conservation activities* for themselves.

8. *Monitor the international wildlife trade* to prevent illegal trade.

9. *Influence public opinion and the policies of governments and private institutions* to promote conservation.

The IUCN, founded in 1949, is the principal scientific advisor to WWF. IUCN continuously reviews and assesses world environmental problems, and promotes research contributing to their solution. It supports a network of volunteer experts who work with the United Nations, WWF, and other important international groups.

IUCN was the first to issue a list of endangered species, called *The Red Data Book*, which is the most reliable source of information about the condition of endangered species around the world.

In 1980 IUCN published a long-range plan for preserving the earth's living resources—the *World Conservation Strategy*. The *World Conservation Strategy* has three major goals: to maintain genetic diversity, ensure that renewable resources remain abundant, and maintain essential ecological processes, such as the way the rain forest recycles carbon dioxide into oxygen.

The Nature Conservancy

For over thirty years, The Nature Conservancy (known as the Conservancy) has taken a different approach to conservation. It has obtained, through outright purchase or gifts, 3.5 million acres in all

Many species of whale are endangered due to relentless hunting by humans. The huge, docile mammals continue to be slaughtered for whale oil.

fifty states, to set aside as wildlife preserve. The Conservancy adds an average of another thousand acres daily. About 1.5 million of these acres are in a thousand Conservancy preserves, the largest private sanctuary system in the world. Thousands of acres more have been turned over to state and national parks and wildlife refuges.

The Conservancy's goal is the preservation of the diversity of living things. In 1974 the Conservancy developed the heritage program, a program that inventories plant and animal populations and rescues those that need assistance.

Developed in South Carolina, the heritage program has proven so successful that every state but Alabama and Arkansas has one. (There is one in the District of Columbia too.) New programs are opening in Canada and in nine Latin American countries. Heritage programs operate on a state-by-state basis as joint programs of the state and the Conservancy.

Under the heritage program, botanists, zoologists, and ecologists take inventory to locate a state's rarest plants, animals, and communities of species. Their information is processed by computers that determine which are most in danger. In a time when controversies and arguments about endangered species are common, the heritage program provides states with information that is up-to-date, unbiased, and reliable about the needs of their endangered species.

Modern arks

Another approach to conservation is taken by zoos and groups that concentrate on keeping individual species on the planet. Rallying to the cry "Extinct is forever!" scientists and zoos use modern technology to revive vanishing species and return them to the wild.

Zoos, once just places to see exotic animals, are the centers of much of this technological skill. In the past, when a zoo wanted a new animal, it just bought one that had been captured in the wild. But, as a growing number of species vanished from their native habitat, zoo officials learned how to breed the animals themselves.

New reproductive technologies and a greater understanding of the needs of exotic animals have enabled zoos to take the lead in saving endangered species.

Zoos learned to cooperate, trading or lending animals across the world to pair individuals that are genetically suited to one another. Pandas, gorillas, and other exotic species are routinely shipped thousands of miles to mate.

Now zoos have gone one step further and applied this kind of careful management to endangered species in the wild. They have become breeding centers for the world's most endangered wildlife, with the goal of returning them to the wild someday.

The San Diego Wild Animal Park, a modern-day Noah's ark for endangered species, operates more than forty-seven captive breeding programs. Occupying almost two thousand acres, it is in the forefront of the U.S. breeding effort. Its breeding programs include the Arabian oryx, Przewalski's horse, Sumatran tiger, South African cheetah, maned wolf, Persian onager, Transcaspian kulan, Somali wild ass, lowland tapir, three species of rhinoceros (East African black, Great Indian, and Northern white), and the California condor.

The park was established in 1973 by the San Diego Zoo, when it found it could not maintain its famous collections. The animals that the zoo sought were dying in their own countries as their habitat was destroyed. The captive breeding program for the Arabian oryx, a species of antelope, has been the San Diego Wild Animal Park's biggest success.

Operation Oryx was no simple matter. The program began over

A rare Arabian oryx and her calf live a sheltered life in the San Diego Wild Animal Park. In its native habitat, its numbers have dwindled to near extinction.

twenty-five years ago. At that time the species had been hunted almost to extinction in the wild. With the support of the newly formed WWF, the Fauna Preservation Society prepared a capture operation in the spring of 1962. Hunting parties had killed sixty-one oryx shortly before the capture group arrived, making the members of the Society wonder if there were any oryx left.

Locating the oryx

Luckily the capture group succeeded in finding three Arabian oryx. But this was not a large enough group for breeding. Another "operation" was planned, this time to find captive oryx in Arabia and zoos. The total came up to ten.

Most of the herd was transferred to the San Diego Zoo. Because there were so few animals to start with, great care was taken to make sure that the breeding program allowed maximum genetic variability. Zoo officials wanted the oryx to have the benefit of as many different genes as possible. By 1977 there were seventy-two oryx in the world, thirty-four of them in San Diego.

In 1978 it was time to separate the herd, to guard against a catastrophic disease wiping out the species. Oryx were shipped to Jordan and Israel. Later shipments went to European zoos. With the future of the oryx in captivity assured, biologists began to think about restoring the antelope to its native land.

With the help of the Sultan of Oman (a country in southeast Arabia) and the enthusiastic support of the native bedu people, two herds of oryx were released into the desert in 1982. Careful scientific monitoring indicates that they are breeding successfully in the wild.

Especially encouraging to conservationists has been the acceptance of the oryx by the bedus. In the time the oryx has lived free on the desert, not one has been harmed by a bedu. Thirty-four Arabian oryx are today living in the wild in Oman, and more will soon be released—a remarkable turnaround from 1962 when the antelope was extinct in nearly all of its former range.

The California condor nearly became extinct in the wild before conservationists captured the last condor in 1987. Fortunately, condors have begun breeding in captivity and are slowly making a comeback.

Perhaps one of the most controversial captive breeding programs aims to save the California condor. In spite of more than thirty years of effort to save these endangered vultures, their number steadily declined until only five breeding pairs and some unmated immature condors survived in the wild.

A captive breeding program began in 1982. At first none of the condor pairs would mate in captivity. However, the program eventually raised thirteen condor chicks hatched from eggs taken from nests in the wild.

In the meantime, disaster struck the condors in the wild. Four of the breeding condor pairs vanished. The Fish and Wildlife Service decided to bring the remaining condors into the captive breeding program before they too disappeared. The last free-flying condor was captured in 1987.

At the time of the capture nobody knew whether condors would breed in captivity. Within a year, two of the newly captured birds became the first California condors to mate in captivity. Their chick, the first California condor bred in captivity, hatched in April 1988. Condor keepers named it Molloko. A second chick hatched in April 1989.

There were twenty-nine California condors in existence in 1989. Scientists hope that the successful rearing of these chicks is one more step down the road to releasing the California condor back into its native habitat.

Molloko, the first California condor to be born in captivity, is fed by a condor puppet. Hatched at the San Diego Wild Animal Park in April 1988, Molloko soon had company when another chick hatched in 1989.

Although no one questions the good intentions of those who are working with the condors, some conservationists look at the steady development of California wilderness and wonder whether the big birds can ever be released into the wild. Is it the future of all endangered species, they ask, to spend their lives in cages?

Although conservation groups may differ in their approach to saving endangered species, each has an important job to do. They are taking responsibility for preserving endangered species. Together they are changing the world.

CHAPTER EIGHT

The Future

In 1980 there were 4.4 billion people on earth. By 1990 there will be 5.2 billion. As more and more people crowd the earth, they fill places where once only animals lived. Forests are cut down, wetlands are drained, and even the ice caps are invaded by pipelines. Wildlife all over the planet is threatened.

At the same time, more and more people realize that something must be done to preserve the earth's vast array of living creatures. Gradually, ways are found to live in harmony with nature. Conservation work in the wild is saving endangered plants and animals, and many countries have created parks and preserves for creatures whose habitat is threatened. There is hope.

Today we are beginning to find the answers to some difficult questions about ourselves and the world we live in. The final answers to those questions will determine what our future will be.

Should every endangered species be saved?

In the United States today a heated debate is going on about how much effort ought to be put into saving members of an endangered species. It would be wrong to think that all those who oppose conservation efforts are insensitive or selfish. There are some times when it might be foolish to try to save a doomed animal. Careful evaluation must be made of the chance for the animal to survive with human help, and return to the wild.

In the fall of 1988, two whales became trapped in the Alaskan ice pack. Day after day people around the world followed their story on television as conservationists tried to free them. Day by day the whales' situation became more desperate as winter set in and the they grew tired. Finally a Soviet icebreaker cleared their way to freedom. The whole world cheered as two weary whales finally made their way through the Alaskan ice pack to the sea. Getting those two trapped whales out of the ice cost over a million dollars, not counting the expenses of the Soviet icebreaker.

Was it worth it *for two whales*? Opinions differ, but in the future we will be faced with more and more of these decisions. *Should we save them or let them die?*

Our decisions may be made with just as much emotion as we felt about the whales. If we choose with our emotions, only cute and cuddly creatures will survive. The pandas will live, but the crocodiles will die. The alternative is to try to maintain a balanced ecosystem, one in which all members of the community have a place.

Pollution

A major problem for the future is pollution. The word pollution might mean car exhaust or smog to many people, but there are other kinds of pollution that are more deadly for wildlife.

DDT is a pesticide used in the 1950s and 1960s to kill insects that attacked farmers' crops. But DDT didn't just affect bugs. It is a nonspecific poison. The poisoned bugs were eaten by robins and starlings, and many of the birds died. Birds of prey, like the peregrine falcon, found the dead birds and fed upon them. Large amounts of DDT were absorbed by the falcons. The DDT caused them to lay eggs with shells so thin that they broke before young falcons could develop. By the time DDT was banned in 1972, not a single breeding peregrine falcon was left alive in the eastern United States.

Luckily, this story has a happy ending. Captive breeding programs have revealed that peregrine falcons settle on tall buildings the way their ancestors nested on tall cliffs. Today falcons can be seen amidst the tall office buildings of Denver, Chicago, Milwaukee, and Salt Lake City, thriving on pigeons and other urban prey. But DDT still remains in our lakes and streams.

Other kinds of pollution poison the earth's rivers, streams, lakes, and oceans. Acid rain falls because of chemicals released into the air by factories burning coal. The rain poisons lakes and rivers many miles away, killing the fish. Even the forests in Europe and North America are slowly being poisoned by acid rain. Oil spills from petroleum tankers pollute the ocean and kill birds along the shore. Garbage from U.S. cities is dumped into the ocean. Radioactive waste

Elephant tusks bring a high price on the black market as precious ivory. Though protected by law, elephants, like their neighbor the rhino, fall victim to human greed and ignorance.

from nuclear reactions is buried underground or dropped into the ocean in large barrels. Each one of these problems must be solved in the future.

Species in jeopardy

Some species may never make a comeback. They have been exploited by humans for so long that there may be no future for them.

Whales, one of the planet's largest mammals, are one of its most endangered species. People have hunted and killed whales for centuries, using their fat for lighting and lubrication. Whale meat is a favorite delicacy in some countries. So many whales have been killed that there may not be enough left to reproduce successfully.

Being useful has caused many species of plants and animals to become extinct, but being beautiful has also brought many species to the verge of extinction. Many exotic animals—the big cats (tigers, snow leopards, and occlots) as well as seals—are endangered because their skins are prized for fur coats. Other colorful animals are collected alive: parrots, tropical fish, exotic snakes, and lizards. Entire hillsides in Central and South America are stripped of vegetation for houseplants to be sent to the United States or Europe.

The elephant may be the next well-known species to disappear. Slaughtered for their ivory tusks, the huge beasts are killed by poachers, 200 each day. Of the 750,000 elephant on the African continent ten years ago, only 20,000 remain.

The poaching problem is complicated by the fact that some ivory is legally sold. Yet conservationists estimate that over 80 percent of the ivory circulating in world trade is illegal. Once the ivory has been carved, it is impossible to determine its origin. World conservation organizations are calling for an immediate end to the ivory trade to save the elephant.

You don't have to be a scientist to help protect endangerd wildlife. You don't even have to leave your home. Here are some ways the World Wildlife Fund suggests to get involved in saving wild things.

These elephant tusks may be used for carvings and jewelry. Elephants continue to be slaughtered for their tusks and so remain seriously endangered.

Learn more about wildlife

Become better informed about wildlife. Start by learning about a specific animal or part of the world. Ask your librarian to recommend books and magazines. Museums and nature centers offer classes that will teach you more.

Let people know how you feel about conserving endangered species. Your letters to members of Congress, the editor of the local paper, and corporate executives can make a difference.

Join a conservation group. There are many different types of conservation organizations. (A few are listed in the back of this book.)

South American poachers skin a jaguar they have killed illegally. The great cat's beautiful coat has been its downfall. Local authorities and conservationists often have difficulty controlling poaching in the jungles where the jaguar lives. Dense vegetation provides hiding places for poachers.

As a member, you can learn more about what needs to be done, and you can help.

Think international. Encourage the conservation group you join to consider the global view of wildlife problems. American organizations can preserve wildlife both here and in other countries. Some groups, like the World Wildlife Fund, work to save habitats worldwide.

Don't buy pets or plants that have been illegally taken from the wild. Before you buy an animal or plant, ask the store if it was bred in captivity or taken from the wild. If the store tells you it was taken from the wild, check to make sure it can be legally sold. Unless you ask questions about exotic plants and animals, the illegal trade will continue.

Don't buy products made of wild animals. Ask if they are made from protected species. If the merchant can't give you a satisfactory answer, don't buy.

When travelling overseas, *refuse to buy protected animal products* such as tortoiseshell. You may be offered such items, but it is illegal to bring them into the United States. If you leave such souvenirs in the marketplace, fewer stores will carry them.

Volunteer. Local museums, nature centers, botanical gardens, zoos, and aquariums allow you to work with experts. Other groups, such as the Boy Scouts, clean up rivers, clear trails, or help nature in other ways.

Make room for wildlife in your own backyard. The plants, insects, and birds that live in your neighborhood need help too.

Share what you've learned. Once you're involved with conserving wildlife, other people will become interested in what you're doing. Make your projects the subject of school reports. Take your friends to the nature center where you volunteer. Your friends will benefit, and so will wildlife.

Glossary

biosphere: All the living species on the earth, and the complex relationships among them.

canopy: The intertwined branches of trees and vines that grow together a hundred feet above the rain forest floor. The canopy protects the rain forest ecosystem from high winds or extreme heat and maintains high humidity inside the forest.

capture programs: Programs for saving endangered species that involve raising the animals in captivity.

captive breeding: Breeding critically endangered species in captivity using modern scientific technology to help them reproduce.

CITES: The Convention on International Trade in Endangered Species of Wild Flora and Fauna, an international treaty that forbids selling or buying any plant or animal that is listed as endangered.

clear cutting: A method of logging that cuts down all the trees in an area.

critical habitat: The areas of land, water, and airspace that a species needs for survival. Critical habitat is protected under the Endangered Species Act of 1973.

critically endangered: A species in immediate danger of becoming extinct because it exists in extremely small numbers. Critically endangered species often must be maintained in captive breeding programs.

delisting: Removing plants and animals protected under the Endangered Species Act from the official list of endangered or threatened species, usually because the species has recovered or has become extinct.

ecosystem: All the living things as well as the soil, air, and water within a habitat.

endangered species: A species that has so few members that it is in danger of dying out.

exotic species: Species that are not native to an area but have been introduced by people.

extermination: Killing off a species.

extinction: Ceasing to exist.

forest litter: Leaves and other organic material that have fallen to the forest floor and are reduced to basic elements. Forest litter provides the nutrients that plants, wildlife, and fish need in order to survive.

genes: The basic units that transmit hereditary characteristics.

genetic diversity: Sharing few hereditary characteristics. In endangered species this is very important, since it protects the species against harmful genes and gives it the greatest possibility of responding to a change in conditions.

habitat: The place that provides everything a plant or animal needs to live and grow.

heritage program: A program developed by The Nature Conservancy to inventory all the endangered species in each state.

listing: Adding a species to the official United States government list of endangered or threatened species according to the provisions of the Endangered Species Act. Listed species are entitled to the full protection of the government, including a complete recovery plan prepared by biologists.

man-eaters: Animals that kill and eat people.

mast: Wild berries, grains, and nuts that have fallen to the forest floor.

migrate: To move from one place to another, usually following changes in the seasons.

native species: Species that occur naturally in an area and have not been imported by people.

nonselective poisons: Poisons whose effects are not limited to one group of animals.

nutrients: The elements needed for the life and growth of plants or animals.

pigeoneers: Hunters who made their living from killing pigeons and shipping them to restaurants and food distributors on the east coast of the U.S.

poachers: People who illegally collect or kill plants or animals.

predator: An animal that lives by killing and eating other animals.

prey: An animal hunted or killed by another animal for food.

range: The home territory of a species.

rulemaking: The formal procedure followed by the Fish and Wildlife Service in determining which species should be placed on the U.S. List of Endangered and Threatened Wildlife and Plants.

selective cutting: A method of logging that cuts only some of the trees in an area. Because the trees and vines in the rain forest support one another, selective cutting may do almost as much damage to the jungle as clear cutting.

silt: Topsoil that has been washed away by heavy rains or flooding.

slash-and-burn: A traditional form of agriculture often used by native peoples in tropical forests. A small plot of land is cleared by cutting down the trees and burning off the underbrush. Because the soil beneath rain forests is usually poor in nutrients, the plot cannot support cultivation for more than a few years and must be abandoned.

species: A group of plants or animals of the same kind that produce young like themselves.

species recovery plan: A plan for saving an endangered or threatened species within the United States. Required by the Endangered Species Act of 1973.

Species Survival Plan: An international plan for saving an endangered species. Biologists and conservationists set goals and consider problems that might arise for the species during the next fifty years.

squabs: Half-grown pigeons.

stand: A technique of killing buffalo developed by commercial hunters. By quietly approaching a small herd and killing the active buffalo one at a time, the hunter kept the animals milling about without stampeding. A single hunter could kill a small herd of buffalo, keeping the carcasses in the same location.

subspecies: A type of animal or plant that differs from others within its species in obvious ways (such as size, color, or form) but still can reproduce with other members of the species.

taxidermist: A person who preserves the skins of fish, birds, and animals, and stuffs them so that they can be displayed.

threatened species: A species that is likely to become endangered.

tropical rain forest: A tall, dense jungle that grows where the equator crosses Asia, Africa, and Latin America.

wallow: A dusty place where animals, such as buffalo, roll in the loose dirt.

water table: The level below which the ground is saturated with water.

Organizations To Contact

African Wildlife Foundation
1717 Massachusetts Ave. NW
Washington, DC 20036

Bureau of Land Management
18th & C Sts. NW
Washington, DC 20240

Caribbean Conservation Corp.
PO Box 2866
Gainesville, FL 32602

Center for Action on
Endangered Species
175 W. Main St.
Ayer, MA 01432

Committee for the Preservation
of the Tule Elk
PO Box 3696
San Diego, CA 92103

Defenders of Wildlife
1244 19th St. NW
Washington, DC 20036

Desert Fishes Council
407 W. Line St.
Bishop, CA 93514

Elsa Wild Animal Appeal
PO Box 4572
North Hollywood, CA 91607

Florida Wildlife Federation
4080 Haverhill Rd.
West Palm Beach, FL 33407

Friends of Animals, Inc.
11 W. 60th St.
New York, NY 10023

International Union for
the Conservation of Nature
Avenue du Mont-Blanc
CH-1196 Gland
Switzerland

National Audubon Society
950 Third Ave.
New York, NY 10022

National Marine Fisheries Service
14th St. and Constitution Ave. NW
Washington, DC 20230

National Park Service
Interior Building
PO Box 37127
Washington, DC 20013-7127

National Wildlife Federation
1400 16th St. NW
Washington, DC 20036-2266

The Nature Conservancy
1815 N. Lynn St.
Arlington, VA 22209

Project Jonah
Box 40280
San Francisco, CA 94140

Sierra Club
730 Polk St.
San Francisco, CA 94109

Society for the Preservation
of Birds of Prey
PO Box 891
Pacific Palisades, CA 90272

U.S. Fish and Wildlife Service
Publications Unit
18th & C Sts. NW
Washington, DC 20240

Wildlife Conservancy
909 12th St., Suite 207
Sacramento, CA 95814

World Wildlife Fund
1250 24th St. NW
Washington, DC 20037

Suggestions for Further Reading

If you want to learn more about the animals and issues described in this book, here are some books that you might enjoy.

Aline Amon, *Orangutan: Endangered Ape*. New York: Atheneum Press, 1977.

M. Banks, *Endangered Wildlife*. Vero Beach, FL: Rourke Corp., 1989.

Olive W. Burt, *Rescued: America's Endangered Wildlife on the Comeback Trail*. Englewood Cliffs, NJ: Julian Messner, 1980.

Jane Burton, *Animals of the Year: The Ecology of East Africa*. New York: Holt, Rinehart and Winston, 1972.

Charles Cadieux, *These Are the Endangered*. San Jose, CA: Stone Walled Press, 1981.

Thomas Cajacob and Teresa Burton, *Close to the Wild—Siberian Tigers in a Zoo*. Minneapolis, MN: Carolrhoda Books, 1986.

Denise Casey, *The Black-Footed Ferret*. New York: Dodd, Mead & Co., 1985.

Barbara Ford, *Wildlife Rescue*. Niles, IL: A. Whitman, 1987.

Paula Hendrich, *Saving America's Birds*. New York: Lothrop Books, 1982.

Linda Koebner, *From Cage to Freedom*. New York: E.P. Dutton, 1981.

Dorothy H. Patent, *Buffalo: The American Bison Today*. Boston: Clarion Books, 1986.

Laurence Pringle, *Wolfman*. New York: Charles Scribner's Sons, 1984.

Miriam Schleen, *Project Panda Watch*. New York: Atheneum Press, 1984.

Jack Denton Scott and Ozzie Sweet, *Little Dogs of the Prairie*. New York: G.P. Putnam & Sons, 1977.

Jack Denton Scott and Ozzie Sweet, *Return of the Buffalo*. New York: G.P. Putnam & Sons, 1976.

John Sidworthy, *A Year in the Life of a Tiger*. Englewood Cliffs, NJ: Silver Burdett, 1987.

Jin Xugi and Markus Kappler, *The Giant Panda*. New York: G.P. Putnam's Sons, 1986.

Index

Picture Credits

Photos supplied by Dixon & Turner Research Associates, Bethesda, Maryland

Cover Photo: Ermanno Vanino, U.S. Fish & Wildlife Service
Tom Cajacob, Minnesota Zoo, 43
© Cresci/Rothco, 18
© Engleman/Rothco, 45
Ron Garrison, Zoological Society of San Diego, 73
Luther C. Goldman, U.S. Fish & Wildlife Service, 15, 63
John Gotischalk, U.S. Fish & Wildlife Service, 62
P. Jackson, World Wildlife Fund-U.S., 41
Library of Congress, 13, 22, 24, 26
Sven-Olof Lindblad, African Wildlife Foundation, 80, 82
© Esmond Bradley Martin, African Wildlife Foundation, 65, 66
Loren McIntyre, 51, 53
Russ Mittermeier, World Wildlife Fund-U.S., 83
National Marine Fisheries Service, National Oceanographic and Atmospheric Association, 70
LuRay Parker © 1985 Wyoming Game and Fish Department, 32
LuRay Parker © 1983 Wyoming Game and Fish Department, 34
LuRay Parker © 1987 Wyoming Game and Fish Department, 35
LuRay Parker © 1988 Wyoming Game and Fish Department, 37
Craig W. Racicot, Zoological Society of San Diego, 76
© Reibrau/Rothco, 61
D. Shane, World Wildlife Fund-U.S., 56
© Carol Simpson/Rothco, 72
Glen Smart, U.S. Fish & Wildlife Service, 75
U.S. Fish & Wildlife Service, 28, 46
R. Weyerhaeuser, World Wildlife Fund-U.S., 64

About the Author

Sunni Bloyd's love of animals began early. Growing up within roaring distance of the Sacramento Zoo, she brought home field mice trapped in her lunchbox and once kept a five-foot-long sand shark in the bathtub for a week. She filled the house with a menagerie of interesting creatures: cats, dogs, hamsters, parakeets, ducks, fish, snakes, butterflies, and even silkworms. Luckily, her mother (who had herself owned a pair of bearcubs as childhood pets) was understanding.

Bloyd earned a B.A. from the University of California at Davis, and a Master's Degree in Education at the University of Dayton in Ohio.

For many years a junior-high-school reading teacher, Bloyd now is an award-winning full-time writer. She, her husband and their two teen-aged sons live in Southern California with only a few cats, two rats, and an old dog.

Acknowledgments

The author would like to express her appreciation to those who provided assistance and information during the preparation of this book:

Tye Roy; Pat Geer; Nancy Ballou; Marilyn Bates; Lynne Tubbe; Richard Block and Ronald L. Tilson, World Wildlife Fund, U.S.; John J. Fay, U.S. Fish and Wildlife Service; Frank S. Todd and Frank Tuey, Sea World; Anne D. Turner, National Wildlife Federation; Laurie Dineen, American Bison Association; Patricia F. Lee, National Buffalo Association; Tom Thorne, Wyoming Game and Fish Department; Defenders of Wildlife; The Nature Conservancy; African Wildlife Foundation; the librarians of Orange County Public Library; and my family.